Angels W

By Johnny Garrison

TABLE OF CONTENTS

PREFACE

Through many years of preaching and ministering to the public, both in the United States and abroad, especially on the African continent, I have seen many strange incidents. Some of them were undoubtedly angelic visitations.

Without question, my life would have ended on numerous occasions had it not been for the special, Heavenly help sent to rescue and deliver us. The angels have truly ministered to me, to my family, and to the worldwide fellowship that we call the Church.

My friends and ministers have requested that these unique, true stories be produced in print, and that's how this work came to be. Our many faithful partners made this book possible.

I pray that this record of angelic help that God has given to us, and to others over the years, will encourage someone who needs help but sees none on their horizon. Have faith in God and believe steadfastly in Him. He has always delivered His children through all generations in the past. He has always delivered us. He will deliver you, too.

1

THE MIRACLE SUIT

We had just returned to West Africa from a one-year furlough. While in the States we gathered many suits of clothes to be taken back to Nigeria, for use by our national pastors. The suits were included in the shipment of our household goods bound for Nigeria. When they arrived, we hung them up in a room in one of the Bible school buildings.

Ministers came from far and wide to select their clothing. We were excited to be able to pass out the "new" clothing to our workers. Their excitement was greater than ours, of course!

First, the National Church Officers made their selections. One of these men, a state presbyter named Stephen, was one of the first Africans I met when I first arrived to begin my missionary work. I particularly wanted to see him blessed with several preaching suits. However, he was a big man. Due to his size, there were very few things he could find to wear among the donated items. He ended up with several pairs of shoes, some dress shirts, one sports coat, a few neckties, and one pair of casual trousers, but that was it. None of the suits were his size!

His disappointment was evident. I felt bad for his sake. I wanted him to have several nice suits as badly as he wanted to own them. Anxiously, he continued trying on suits until he had gone through all that remained several times. There just weren't any suits found that fit him. He kindly offered his thanks to us for what he had received and made his way back a full day's journey to his home. He made no complaint about his disappointment at not obtaining even a single suit of clothes. This man was a real Christian gentleman.

Stephen usually came to the Bible school only once a month for a district board meeting, so I didn't expect to see him until the next end-of-the-month meeting. Two days later he showed up at the mission house. He said he had to speak to me. It surprised us to see him so soon. We commented, concerning his unexpected appearance.

He calmly replied that he had come for his new suit!

Surprised, I asked, "What suit?"

He answered, "Last night while I was sleeping, your mother (who was helping with the distribution of the clothing), appeared in my dream and told me to come back to the mission. She said she had found a suit that would fit me. So, I have come for my suit," he concluded.

Somewhat embarrassed about the situation, I remembered how hard he had tried to find a suit that fit. I advised him that there were no new clothes added to the ones he had already tried. He insisted, though, that his suit was ready for him to pick up, saying, "I remember what it looks like. Your mother showed it to me in my dream."

I knew that Mother had not found a suit that would fit him. None of us at the mission had placed a suit there for him. Despite this knowledge, it was useless to discuss it further, so I turned and headed to the storage room. We entered the room and he immediately walked over to the rack where he said my mother had placed "his" suit.

He found the suit he had seen in his dream and lifted it off the rack. As he held it up for us all to see, he excitedly said, "This is the one!" He tried it on and the most amazing thing happened. The suit fit him as though tailor-made for him!

The Lord, by his Spirit, spoke to me and reminded me of what he said many years ago:

> "And why take ye thought for raiment? Consider the lilies of the field, how they grow; they toil not, neither do they spin: And yet I say unto you, that even Solomon in all his glory was not arrayed like one of these. Wherefore, if God so clothe the grass of the field, which today is, and tomorrow is cast into the oven, shall He not much more clothe you, oh ye of little faith?" (Matthew 6:28 - 30)

Pastor Stephen received a suit "tailor-made" by God's hand. A ministering angel went on a shopping trip to collect a special gift for one of the Lord's special servants. Or, the Lord Himself miraculously placed that suit on the rack. Decide for yourself!

What really happened we won't know until Heaven reveals its secrets. Regardless, it was a "miracle suit". How it arrived and who put it there remains a mystery!

This unique story does not end at that! A ministers' conference was underway in Abak, in Cross River State, Nigeria. Brother Stephen was present, wearing his "Miracle Suit". Present with him at the services were many of what are now the national leaders of the Nigerian church.

Brother Stephen seemed unusually heavy in spirit and was somewhat troubled. At the closing of one evening service, he went from minister to minister, laying his hands on each of the converts he had won. He prayed specifically for each one of them, and the Holy Spirit touched and moved on each of them as he ministered to them in his prayers.

When this giant of a saint finished praying for the last of his converts, he moved toward the edge of the platform and turned his face toward the wall. He raised his hands up in the air as far as they would go, and with outstretched arms towards heaven, he continued praying mightily in the Spirit. Tears flowed down his cheeks like twin rivers, with great drops of tears falling from his lower face.

Suddenly a massive heart attack hit Brother Stephen, and in

a short moment, he was gone from this life forever. Great effort was made to revive him. We tried everything we could think of, in addition to intense, intercessory prayer. But he was gone from among us.

It was a most sad time. All who attended the conference were stunned beyond words. However, everyone knew that if any human being had ever made it to the Heavenly Kingdom, Brother Stephen was surely and quickly granted entrance. His life was full of godliness and good works.

The final note of the story is quite wonderful. We all remained at the meeting until the funeral was concluded. It was a very simple, but fitting farewell to a very fine Christian man. A loyal soldier of the Cross. No under-shepherd was ever more trustworthy or served more faithfully in the ranks of God's Army than Brother Stephen.

No finer tribute could be paid him than to be buried in his "Miracle Suit".

2

TEKLEMARIAM SEES THE ANGEL

Brother Teklemariam came to Nigeria, West Africa, to preach at the Annual Ministers Conference. From that meeting, we were scheduled to go to another Ministers Conference in Cameroon.

Regional Field Supervisor for Africa, Reverend. J. P. Hughes, and his wife, June, were in the meetings. They were to accompany Brother Teklemariam, his wife, Peggy, and I. Also attending were missionary Paul Suber and his family, from Ivory Coast.

The Ministers Conference was a great monument to the growth of the church in Nigeria. Many blessed events occurred at the Nigerian Conference. Because the Nigerian conference went so well, everyone was excited and looking forward to what was going to take place in the Cameroon Ministers Conference. However, all of us were dreading the long, hot trip, and the ever-present insects. It was at least a twelve hour ride. Because it was the dry season, the journey would not be treacherous, as it would have been had the trip been made during the rainy season.

The major problem we would face besides the heat and insects was the bumpy dirt roads full of huge ruts left by the many trucks that regularly traveled that road. During the rainy season, many of them could not make it through but remained stuck in calf-deep mud for several days until the roads dried out.

Our two-truck mini-caravan left before daylight and had an enjoyable trip all day despite the heat and bugs. There were lots of vehicles on the road coming and going during the year-end holidays.

As evening approached, clouds begin to gather. Usually, they passed without rain. But this day, there was a sudden downpour. Rain pelted down very hard for quite some time. The rough road we were traveling on turned almost instantly into a huge, very slippery, sea of mud.

We were traveling in a four-wheel drive, all-terrain type truck, so it was not too difficult to negotiate around two-wheel drive vehicles that rapidly became bogged down in the mud. The roads were in the foothill country of Mount Cameroon, so not much progress was being made as the rain continued. We were only about two-thirds of the way along our journey as night begin to fall. Travel slowed to a crawl.

In a valley, we suddenly came upon a large number of two-wheel drive vehicles stuck in the mud along the road. The road was totally blocked. There was no way to pass.

The trip thus far had consumed the twelve hours allotted for the whole trip, and all the travelers were weary. The vehicles were stopped, and parties from both of our trucks walked forward to the road block to see if there was a remedy for the situation.

The road was blocked at a place where some road construction had been done and rushing water from the hard rains had backed up into a large lake. The water was rushing under a temporary metal culvert, over which the road passed. The traffic tie-up was right on top of the culvert. Several cars were buried in mud up to their car frames.

Our two drivers quickly assessed the situation. They decided to try to push one of the buried vehicles out of the way so the others could pass over the culvert. None of our party wanted to sleep in our four-wheeler pickups on this road!

There was no way but to dismount and walk through the mud, which was extremely slick and up to our calves. Walking gingerly did little to help. We waded out into the mud to push back the car that was blocking everyone. In a short time, we pushed his vehicle back far enough for our four-wheelers to pass him by. But as we returned to our vehicles to pass him, he hurriedly drove back down to the culvert. And he promptly bogged down again!

This happened several times – we would push him back and return to our vehicles to mount up, so we could pass him and go over the culvert. Each time he gunned his engine and drove back to the same spot, only to be stuck again! Others were helping us to push him back. After seeing him pull this antic several times, they refused to help him, or us, again.

Finally, I went to the man and said that everyone was tired of his actions, and if he moved his vehicle back into the way again, I was going to use our four-wheel drive truck with the large tires and just climb over his vehicle to go on. I thought that saying this would persuade him to remain where we had pushed him out of the way.

He calmly looked at me and said, "What did you say, white man?"

When I heard him use those terms, and with an attitude, I stopped and looked around. While looking around I realize that there were three white men among a large crowd of angry Africans. We were out in the jungle, in the dark of night, many miles away from any justice. We stood little chance getting out alive if trouble came...

Immediately I apologized to him. He also calmed down. We pushed him back one more time, then. With this final push, he became stuck and could no longer move his car. At last, he was out of the way enough for us to try to pass him!

We slowly started to pass him. But suddenly we entered a deep rut and our vehicle almost slid over into his car. I couldn't go forward without hitting his car and starting a riot, so I began back away from his car. The vehicle behind me, however, had their bright lights on and I could barely see anything because of the reflection of the bright lights.

Moving slowly because of the mud, the wheels of our vehicle suddenly caught traction and started to move backward. After I moved away from the angry man's car, our truck being sliding sideways, toward a ravine on the edge of the culvert.

Brother Suber was blowing his horn behind me. They all had their windows down and were shouting to us. But as our truck began to tip off the road into the ravine, it swiftly lurched to a halt.

Managing carefully to turn the motor off, I crawled out of our vehicle. What I saw as I looked at our truck caused me to freeze in my tracks! The lights of Brother Suber's truck permitted me to see that we were about to fall off the road, upside down, into the rushing waters of the ravine. Carefully slithering back to our truck, I quietly urged the others inside to gently get out of my side of the truck. As I cautioned them not to move suddenly, but as quietly and carefully as they could, I realized they did not understand the dangerous situation.

When all were safely out, and we had moved back from the edge of the ravine, we began to discuss what had really happened.

Brother Suber said that he could see us sliding off into the rushing waters and was trying to alert us to the danger by blowing his horn and yelling at us.

Brother Teklemariam was in the vehicle with Brother Suber, and he began to urgently intercede in prayer for us. Suddenly,

Brother Teklemariam said he saw a big angel move quickly to the ravine side of our truck, spread his arms wide, and place his hands on the truck to hold the vehicle so it would not fall into the rushing flood waters.

A praying man, a faithful and merciful Living God, and His protecting angels had crushed the plan of Satan to destroy the key ministries of these great missionary supervisors and their wives. Because of God's intervention through the big angel, these two important African nations continued to experience great revival harvest of souls.

3

SHOW ME THE WAY TO GO HOME

It was again the rainy season. We left home at 5 a.m. to travel six hours from where we lived in Abak, Cross River State, Nigeria, West Africa, to Port Harcourt, a large city about 80 miles away. The purpose of our trip was to purchase groceries. We were going to buy a month's supply of food for our family.

Rain fell most of the day. Under normal conditions travel on the Nigerian roads was difficult. But when it rained, passage was almost impossible. It was a difficult trip just to reach Port Harcourt, but the return trip home was very bad because of the continuous rain.

Darkness started to fall. We were still only about halfway home when all traffic on the road stopped. At a point, we sat without moving for an hour. I decided to exit our vehicle and walk forward to learn why the traffic was stopped. I learned that a big truck and turned over. It was lying on its side, in the middle of the road, up ahead of our car.

When I returned to our vehicle, I backed up our car out of the traffic jam, to a nearby junction, then stopped to assess our situation. We did not have money for a hotel, even if one had been available – which there wasn't. We could not go back to the city where we had just completed our grocery shopping. We didn't have a place to stay there, either. We were stuck in a hopeless traffic jam, at least 40 miles away from home, with night almost totally upon us.

The children were hungry and very tired from a long day of activity. It was unsafe for us even to try to sleep in the car; thieves and robber bands were always serious, life-threatening realities. Or, if thieves and robbers didn't find us, the mosquitoes and swarms of every type of flying and crawling insect you can imagine would eat us up during the night.

Again, stepping outside the car, I begin to pray that the Lord would help show us the way out of this predicament. It was while I was pacing back and forth, praying, that a long black Mercedes-Benz car pulled up alongside me. The back window rolled down and the voice of an African spoke into the night to me.

The voice asked, "Are you from Abak, Cross River State?"

I quickly answered, "Yes!"

The person behind the yet faceless voice asked, "Would you like for me to show you the way home?"

Again, I quickly answered "Yes!"

While I answered him outwardly, I knew in my heart that it

was impossible because the only road toward home was blocked hopelessly by a sea of mud from the constant rains, the traffic jam, and the overturned truck in the middle of the washed-out road.

Without further discussion, the voice said, "Follow me."

I jumped back into my car and started to follow his lead. Immediately I realized, however, that he was not traveling in the direction of our home! I followed him for a few miles when he suddenly turned off onto a small dirt road. He wound around on the small road until the road finally played out.

Another voice began to speak to me – the voice of doubt, upbraiding me for following an African stranger, especially at night. You have made a mistake for sure. You have fallen into a big trap. This car you are following will stop in a few minutes, block the road, rob and kill you and your family. You will be left where no one will be able to find you.

Immediately, the peace of the Lord flooded my spirit and soul. The voice of the Holy Spirit spoke calmly to me, "Follow him. He is taking you home."

The black Mercedes drove across farms, through residential yards, and places where there were no roads at all. After about an hours' time, we came to a tee in the road, and we were suddenly back on the paved road again. After a few minutes on the paved road, I realized we were on a familiar road-- it was the road to our home!

As if to say, "You are all right now," the Mercedes begin to sound its horn repeatedly, as a signal to us. Off into the dark African night, it sped away, disappearing rapidly. We never saw it again.

When we finally made it home, we were very tired, hungry, and sleepy, but we were alive and safe. Our hearts were really singing to the tune, All day, all night, angels watching over me, My Lord. All day, all night, angels watching over me!

In the days following this incident, I attempted to retrace our journey on that dark night. To my knowledge, and by the knowledge of others who lived in those areas, there is no other way to travel to miss the area where the traffic jam and accident had occurred.

Was it an angel in the car? All we know for sure is that the Lord has said that if we acknowledge Him in all our ways, He will direct our paths.

Praises unto our God forever!

4

MIRACLE BABY

Traveling in the State of Texas, the Africa Impact Team was due to stop at a church in Mont Belvieu. Just before church was to begin that evening, the pastor was called out because of a death.

As a normal practice, when the pastor is not present, I do not preach. Instead, the Impact Team members each testified. The last member to testify invited everyone to the altar to pray.

While everyone was praying, I felt the leading of the Holy Spirit directing me to pray for a young lady who appeared to be in her early twenties. As I place my hands on her head and started to pray, the Spirit of Prophecy came upon me.

The Word of the Lord said through me, to the young woman, "You have been faithful, and I have seen your tears. Therefore, I will take away your reproach and I will give you a child. When he is born, people will say that the Lord surely has done a great thing. Be not afraid to go on your way, for I, the Lord, have spoken this to you, my child."

The young lady started sobbing, weeping so pitifully before the Lord, but worshiping God all the while. It wasn't until after the service was over and we were visiting with the some of the saints that one of them told the team members that this young lady could not have children. She had tried before, complications had set in, and it was not possible for her to have a child because part of her female organs had been surgically removed. She was, of course, very excited that the Lord had told her she would have a child. But many wondered if it was even possible.

The Africa Impact Team left Mont Belvieu, continuing their travels. Several months later, while visiting the Because of the Times Conference in Alexandria, Louisiana, we again met this young lady. She was accompanied by her husband. They happily informed us that she was expecting. We all rejoiced at what the Lord had done! He never fails. All His promises are true and right!

Sometime later, I received an urgent telephone call that this same sister was having serious complications in her pregnancy. It appeared she was not going to be able to deliver the child.

When the Impact Team received this report, they entered into intercessory prayer on her behalf, seeking God's intervention. It was while we were thus praying for her that the Lord spoke to me saying, "Call her. Tell her that I will send an angel to be with her until the child is born. My Messenger will keep the enemy pushed back until the time of the delivery is past."

After prayer, I called her. Brokenhearted and fearful, she poured out her story of what had happened. She said she had wanted to have a baby girl, but that the ultrasound tests showed that the child would be a boy. She became so disappointed and depressed that dire complications began to develop. She was quickly taken back to her doctor.

After his examination, he informed her that she had tumors or small growths on her female organs. He could not tell her for sure that she would be able to deliver her child. Since that visit to the doctor, she had been deeply depressed, afraid that she would lose her child.

When she stopped talking, I spoke and told her what the Lord had said to me while the Impact Team was in prayer about her situation. Suddenly, while I was speaking to her over the telephone, a "presence" entered her life. All of her depression immediately lifted when her angel arrived.

She went back to the doctor, this time accompanied by the Angel of the Lord. By the same unexplainable means the doctor's diagnosis changed. This time the doctor seemed to feel the tumors would help her in her delivery. With confidence, the lady faced the remaining term of her pregnancy.

Only a short time later, a baby boy was born. He was very healthy, and handsome!

The Africa Impact Team was blessed to be able to attend the church service where a jubilant mother and father gladly gave their "Miracle Son" back to the Lord, dedicating his life to God's service.

Anthony Brent Coots was the name given to this miracle baby boy. He is a very special child!

5

THE ANGEL AND THE GLORY TRAIN

The dedication to the Lord of baby Anthony Brent Coots was a special occasion for us, so we were in Texas to attend the event. While attending that service there, this testimony was shared with me.

Sister Terri Coots' aunt was on her way to church with her mother-in-law and her two-year-old daughter. The pickup truck that her aunt was driving stalled directly on a set of railroad tracks at a crossing. When the train whistled its approach to the crossing, the danger was imminent!

The mother-in-law had a severe medical problem with her legs. She couldn't move very fast, so she opened the truck door, fell outside the truck onto the ground, and rolled away from the truck to safety.

Sister Terri's aunt could not get the seat belt release mechanism to work, so the little girl was stuck in the truck. She tried frantically to release her baby, but to no avail. The approaching train whistle was wailing loudly as the train rapidly bore down on the stalled truck. When the mother saw she could not release her daughter from the safety belt, she slammed the truck door shut, screamed "Jesus!" and she ran for safety. He was her only hope as this massive train slammed into the pickup truck that held her small child prisoner, trapped because of a faulty seat belt. Metal screeched and groaned from the impact!

The train slammed the truck down the tracks a distance, where the truck then lurched off the train rails and rolled down a steep hill, baby still strapped inside. After the train passed, the baby's mother dashed madly toward the smashed, mangled truck. When Sister Terri's aunt reached the vehicle and looked inside, however, the child appeared to be all right! Miraculously, she had suffered no injuries, not even a scratch.

An onlooker called the rescue squad and an ambulance picked up the mother, her child, and the mother-in-law, and carried all three to the local hospital. Emergency room staff examined them all in the emergency room, but they appear unharmed, so they were released and sent home.

The very next day the little girl was sitting on the couch with her father. She suddenly spoke up and said to him, "Daddy, let's have church."

She asked her father to "testify" first. He quietly thanked the Lord that his daughter, wife, and mother were saved from the horrible accident with the train. It was obvious his heart was touched. Then he asked the little girl to testify. She really startled her father with what she said. The little girl thanked the Lord for "that beautiful sister" that was in the truck with her when the train hit the truck. She said that the sister

riding in the truck with her took the steering wheel and turned that truck away from that "Glory Train."

As a little girl testified, the mother working in the kitchen heard her words. The mother ran quickly into the room where the girl was testifying.

She said, "Baby, no one was in the truck with you. Grandmother and I had to get out."

Her innocent little face shone brilliantly as she turned it up towards her mother. With her face shining like an angel's, the child again told of the beautiful sister who was in the truck with her. The little girl continued with her story saying, "She had beautiful long hair!"

Puzzled, the mother asked the girl if she knew the name of the "sister."

Quickly the girl replied, "Sister Donna."

"But, baby," the mother urged, "we don't know anybody by that name."

The small girl replied, "Yes we do, mommy, because sometimes I see her in the prayer room at church."

At the dedication of Anthony Coots, the girl's mother spoke publicly of this incident. She said that she did not know who that "sister" really was, but that maybe she really was Sister Terri's Angel. Sister Terri's aunt gave thanks to God that the "sister" was in the truck with her little girl on the day of the accident.

However, the story continued to unfold. The pastor of the church went to look at the truck the day after the accident. He said there was a small basket of apples on the seat next to where the little girl was trapped. He said that all the windows of the truck with broken out, but that where the child had been sitting, there was not even one single piece of shattered glass! The pastor looked closer at the apples. He discovered that the apples were full of fragmented pieces of glass, as if someone had pressed all the glass fragments into the apples.

The child had no cuts or scratches anywhere on her, as the emergency room personnel certified during their examination! So, what happened to the glass fragments upon impact from the train? Had an angel of the Lord caught each fragment of broken glass that came near the child in an apple? Surely the Lord is still a miracle working God!

6

ANGELS IN THE FAST LANE

On this Sunday evening, we were in Florida on furlough, doing deputation travel to raise our budget for our next term of appointment in Nigeria, West Africa. When the service ended we were going to drive all night to southern Louisiana, because I was scheduled to speak there the next night at a special meeting.

We finished our fellowship with the pastor and his family in Florida a little after midnight. Then we were on our way to Louisiana.

There wasn't very much traffic on the roads during the night hours. I was quickly bored with the night driving. I was already very tired. Soon I was struggling to stay awake. My family was already asleep. Their restful state beckoned me, but I knew I had to drive all night to keep our schedule.

I encountered some heavy patches of fog along the interstate highway. When driving in these intermittent patches, I had to slow down to make sure I didn't go off the road or hit another vehicle. Even the hot coffee I had with me didn't break the monotony of this trip. The weather was deteriorating rapidly, which made the trip worse, too. Yet I struggled alone, pressing towards Louisiana.

Suddenly there were headlights behind me, rushing quickly up behind us. My first reaction was to check to make sure I wasn't speeding, in case the car behind us was a patrol car. I surely didn't want or need a speeding ticket!

The car coming from behind quickly caught us and zoomed past. It was an older model Chevrolet Caprice. The car had no license plate on it. It had a very dark tinting on all the windows, but I could still see what I thought were four young black men, wearing baseball caps turned backward on their heads. They were slumped down, with their heads resting on the backs of the seats. They look like they were all asleep, including the driver!

They struck me as funny. They looked so relaxed that I started laughing. Then, when I was laughing, I started waking up. Looking at them, I decided to catch them, and stay with them to watch them some more. I began driving very fast, trying to catch up with them. Somehow, no matter how fast I went, they stayed ahead of me and I could not catch them. At times I could only see their tail lights ahead of me.

I took my foot off the accelerator and our car started slowing down after I looked down to see how fast we were traveling, trying to catch that Chevy. But the thought came to me that at least I was wide awake and alert, trying to tail them.

Watching them, when I could get close enough, was good for another laugh, I thought. Off after them we sped.

It seemed that they knew the road well. I figured they must have been local boys, especially because of the skillful way they maneuvered through the tunnel in Mobile, Alabama, and all the curvy roads near there. I could barely see anything, but their driver seemed to have eyes everywhere in his head. For him, there seemed to be no problem seeing the fog covered road. With the heavy fog patches that totally soaked in some areas of the roads, I felt better following their tail lights. Tired as I was, though, it never occurred to me until we had passed through three states that they could not have been local people.

Just before daybreak, we saw a police car blocking the interstate up ahead of us. There was an accident. After stopping, I got out of our vehicle and moved ahead on foot to find out what it happened.

The police officer I encountered said there was a vehicle on fire up ahead and that all traffic would have to wait for a fire truck that was on its way to the scene. Traffic began to back up, and we were stuck in the jam. It seemed evident that we would have to wait it out.

I decided it was time for a much-needed nap! When traffic resumed, I was refreshed, and we completed our trip in record time. Following those tail lights at such high speeds had paid off in getting to Louisiana ahead of our scheduled arrival time.

The next day, while in casual conversation, someone told us about a horrible accident that had taken place the night before on the Interstate at Mobile, Alabama.   About 150 cars had piled up in the accident caused by heavy night fog which had completely covered the interstate on which we had just traveled. We were told that many people had been killed and many more injured in the melee!

Our hearts were heavy for the injured and those suffering the loss of loved ones, but then a realization hit me!

No wonder that Chevy Caprice had swept through the curvy roads and tunnel in Mobile in such an expert fashion! All I had done was to follow the car' s tail lights, moving exactly as they did, even in the same lanes in which they had traveled! That old Chevy had swept in and out of the different interstate lanes as though he had perfect night vision!

As I listened to the report from our friends, my spirit began to sing the old, familiar song "...Angels watching over me, my Lord!"

It wasn't just some local boys out for a spin in their old car, but angelic guides who delivered us safely through the dangerous night, and the awesome crash site, to our distant point so we could do the work and will of our Lord Jesus Christ!

7

FIGHT AT THE ROAD BLOCK

Once, a fellow missionary from another church organization accompanied me to Port Harcourt to bring home a shipment of supplies for our mission station. The journey had been long, but things went smoothly. There was a little traffic because it was very early when we left home.

On the return trip home, we were moving slowly because we were escorting a big tractor and trailer that carried a 20-foot steel sea container with our shipment of goods inside. At around the halfway point on the return trip, I noticed that there seemed to be less traffic than normal. As we traveled, people occasionally run out to the road to try to flag us down. I thought they were just wanting a ride. Then suddenly the truck driver stopped the big rig. I backed up to see why he had stopped. When I reached him, he had entered a small roadside store.

The driver finally emerged from the store. He turned off the lights and motor of the big truck. Then he walked over to my vehicle and said, "I am not going any further. There is trouble on the road up ahead, and these people in the store are advising me not to try to go any further up the road."

I tried to persuade him to continue, but he again said he would not go any further. I told him there was no trouble on the road because we had traveled over the road that morning. The driver flatly refused to travel on any further on the road. I saw it was useless to try to talk to him. Then I told him to stay with the truck. I was going to go up the road to the state line police station to make sure everything was alright. He waited while I went.

I didn't see anything unusual or out of the ordinary along the way and finally reached the police station. I inquired about any problems that might have occurred along the road. The officer-in-charge informed me that there were some disputes at the state border earlier in the day.

The argument seemed to be between two opposing Villages along the state line, but nothing has been confirmed in the report that the officer had received. When I told the officer in charge about a driver being afraid to drive the truck and trailer into the area, he offered to send two police officers in our car with us to escort the truck and our vehicle to the police station.

The two officers followed me back to the truck. After some discussion, they persuaded our driver to follow them back to the police station. By this time, it was after midnight. As we caravanned with the police escort towards the state border and police station, I could see movement alongside the road ahead. When things came clearly into focus I discovered a large log across the road. We were forced to come to a complete stop.

Suddenly we were surrounded by what appeared to be hundreds of armed villagers. Many of them were heavily drugged. Many were also very drunk.

They jerked open our vehicle doors and tried to drag us out of our vehicles. The two police officers escorting us to safety left my car and fled on foot into the jungle. We never saw them again!

The mob began to shout, "We are going to kill you!"

I kept asking what was wrong. I told them that we were missionaries and that we had nothing to do with any trouble in the area. They answered by informing us that there had been a border dispute that day and that people, many people on both sides of the dispute had been killed. They had pledged to their Village that any cars with out-of-state license plates passing through the area would be stopped. The passengers were to be killed on site and their vehicles burned.

Unfortunately, our Sheaves for Christ vehicle had out-of-state plates on it. It seemed that there was nothing I could say to dissuade them from their purpose, try as I might, and try I did! We were in deep trouble. It appeared that we would most certainly die within the next few minutes.

The mob began pointing their guns towards us. Those nearest us put their gun barrels in our faces and prepared to open fire on us. They screamed at us and started pulling their triggers. But every gun they tried to fire jammed. No bullets through their barrels. Growing angrier, they grabbed us and dragged us from our vehicle. Cursing at us, they begin to hit us. In a split-second, a spirit of peace came over me. I knew something was about to happen, we were about to receive divine help!

Out of nowhere, it seemed, a very large black man elbowed his way to the side of our vehicle. This large black man grabbed the man who was holding me, hit him with his fist, and knocked him flat on the ground with one blow.

Our defender yelled to the mob, "Leave my missionary alone!"

With that yell, he leaped into the middle of the angry crowd and started fighting them. He pushed them back, by sheer brute force, clearing a way for us to re-enter the vehicle. He opened the door for us, told us to hurry and get in, and to follow him.

How he moved the tree blocking the road, commandeered a vehicle from the mob, and roared off into the night down the road, still puzzles me when I think about it. This man seemed like a one-man army! We were only too glad to follow. Even that cantankerous truck driver was happy to get on down that road!

Our deliverer led us back to the police station, got out of his captured vehicle, and walked over to my car. He told me I would be safe now.

The officer-in-charge came out and begin to question us about what had happened. After telling him the story of our deliverance I turned to introduce the big man who helped us, but he was gone, as was his commandeered car. I didn't notice when he left, and no one heard his vehicle leave.

No one knew anything about the commandeered vehicle. No one saw the man who helped us but my missionary friend who made the trip with me, and the truck driver. We never found the vehicle he used to lead us away from the angry mob, and we never saw our helper again.

The truck driver went to a hotel for the night. The truck stayed at the police station that night. The missionary friend and I drove home to our mission stations and families, safe and sound.

The stories we heard at home were not at all pleasant, however. Homes, properties, and many vehicles were devastated in the very area where we had been stopped. Worse, more than 250 persons had been murdered! It had been a very serious day.

Despite the bad news, my heart could not help but soar in song to God: "All day, all night, angels watching over me, my Lord!"

Do I really believe in angels? Yes, I most certainly do! We know that they are not to be worshipped, however, the Bible teaches us about them. On numerous occasions, I have experienced them. I know for certain that my life would have ended long ago had it not been for their direct intervention.

Lord, I do believe. And if I ever falter, Lord, please help thou my unbelief.

For the many deliverances at the hands of these ministering spirits, I say humbly, thank you! Thank you! Thank you, Jesus!

8

THE ANGEL ON MAMA'S CAR

My mama is one of the godliest mothers you'll ever meet. I am greatly blessed to have such a wonderful mother. She raised me right and always lived the kind of life in front of me to keep her Godly testimony pure. She helped me to understand that God must always be first in our lives and taught me many other valuable lessons also.

My father died during our first term of service as missionaries in Africa. It was a blessed time for me to be able to make it home in time to be with him before he passed from this life. Thanks to the wonderful understanding and cooperation of my leaders in Africa, and all of the Foreign Missions Division at our headquarters, I was able also to help with his funeral and burial.

After he died I was faced with the responsibility of caring for Mama. This weighed very heavily on me and she sensed what I was feeling. A few days after Dad was buried, Mama found me alone one day and opened up the subject, saying what only a mother can say and make it stick.

She carefully looked at me and with a quiet assurance in her spirit that I didn't feel yet, said, "Son don't worry about me. I'll be all right. You go on back to Africa and do the work that the Lord has called you to do. Many years ago, I gave you to God to do his work, and you must go and do it. I will trust the Lord. God will take care of me," she finished.

I really didn't want to leave her, but I knew that the African work was waiting for me. We both knew that it was the will of God for my life at that time. But it was one of the hardest things I ever had to do - leaving my mom alone after my dad passed away. It took something out of me that left an empty spot for a long, long time.

Mama lived alone most of the time, during the years that followed. But she continued to be faithful to her church in Charlotte, North Carolina. Her pastor was and is a great friend of mine, Reverend David Elms. The church he pastors is the one that I pastored before going to Africa as a missionary. Mama stayed at our home church. Mama was active in her church while still working a secular job to support herself. She was in her mid-seventies when the incident I'm writing about occurred.

Mama's one-way drive to church was about 30 minutes. That drive included passing through some very rough areas and neighborhoods. While she was at church one night, there had been some racial violence, along with a lot of major destruction, in an area she drove through each time she went to and from the church. She had no knowledge of what had happened in that area. But she was headed right through the troubled area on her way home from the church service that night! Some muggings and rapes

occurred while people were driving through the area. Several women were dragged from their cars as they passed through the troubled area.

Even though mama had a car phone, graciously provided out of deep love and concern by her pastor sometime before this incident occurred, her sister was unable to reach her by her cell phone to tell her what was occurring in the area. Her sister also tried to call the church before mama left the service to warn her to take another route on the way home. When the call came from her sister, mama had already left the church, and she missed the warning. The frantic calls to her car phone did not go through. It was very strange because the area usually enjoyed excellent car phone reception.

On the trip home, mama sensed a beautiful afterglow of the presence of the Holy Ghost from the service she had just attended. The Holy Ghost seemed to fill the car, it was so close and so real. As she traveled through the area of the trouble, she did not even recognize the debris and aftermath of destruction from the violence and racial disturbances which had rocked that section of the city. She remembered only concentrating on the sweet presence of the Lord filling her car as she drove home.

When she arrived safely at her home she learned what had happened in the area she had just driven through. What amazed her even more, was that the troubles were still going on, and she had just driven right through them without experiencing any problems! Mama rejoiced in the Lord and thanked Him for seeing her through the rough areas safely, and calmly went on to bed.

It was sometime later, while she was traveling home from another church service, on the same route, that she began to think about what had happened when those troubles occurred. As she was praising the Lord for his divine protection, she began to talk to God about the specific incident. She was talking to the Lord about it, thanking Him, when the Holy Spirit of the Lord suddenly spoke to her, saying, "Look in your side mirror."

Mama looked in the mirror and got a huge shock and surprise! She saw the wings of an angel that was apparently riding on top of her car, with his wings wrapped across the top and down the sides. The wings of the angel almost completely covered the car as she sped along on her way home from church.

The Lord spoke to her again, and said, "This is what happened that night and every night when you drive home. You are protected by my guardian angels, day and night, wherever you go. I have given them charge over you. Fear not, for I am with you, and I am able to protect you in all situations!"

At the time of this writing, mama is now 77 years young, still making the 30-minute drive each way to her church, still rejoicing in the Lord, she is unafraid, enjoying His Divine protection.

God is so good! And he's good all the time!

9

THE DRUNK SOLDIER

The day had been tiring. We had traveled some bad and dangerous roads to finally arrive in another state, where we were conducting a crusade. We finally arrived in the late afternoon. We prepared for the meeting. During the service, we enjoyed the good move of God's great Spirit. With such a move underway, the services lasted late.

The treacherous journey home was in the dark. It was complicated by the fact that we needed to extend the trip a bit in order to drop off some local area pastors at their homes on our way home. At the home of one of our pastors, we learned that there had been trouble in the city that day. A curfew had been ordered by the city officials. The only source of reliable communication was the radio, but we had not been on the channel listening while we were in service that night. We realized quickly that we were violating the curfew. No people or vehicles were on the streets. The state was under direct military rule. Soldiers represented the "on-the-spot" authority, and they could shoot any lawbreakers at their discretion.

Thinking that the proper answer to getting ourselves off the streets was to hurry up and get on home, we continued to travel, trying to get the last pastor to his home before we ran into trouble. We finally arrived at the pastor's home. Dropping him off, we started on our 40-mile journey to our home. We had not gone even one mile when we were stopped by a roadblock. The soldier at the roadblock was heavily intoxicated.

Since we were fairly new in the country, we had little command of the local language. With only my wife and I and our two small children in the car, our communication ability was very poor.

The soldier who stopped us, told us that we were breaking the curfew law, and could be shot on sight by any soldiers finding us. I quietly shared with him that we were conducting a crusade and had not heard the news of the trouble, learning of the curfew only a few miles back at the other minister's house. I tried to help him see that we couldn't prevent being on the road. We were certainly trying to get off the road!

At the mention of the Crusade, the soldier became very animated. He started cursing at me and aimed his automatic rifle at my head! He ordered me to get out of the car. He shouted that he was going to make me roll in the mud and water before he shot me!

He was waiting for me to respond to his order to get out of the car, when suddenly my wife shouted very loudly, "In Jesus name!"

An amazing look of utter terror came over the drunk soldier's face as he suddenly staggered backward from our vehicle. It was as though someone had given him a mighty push to drive him away from my vehicle. While he was staggering, trying to figure out what had happened to him, I hurriedly started our vehicle, threw the gearbox in forward gear, and floored the gas pedal. You can be sure we watched through the rear-view mirror and back window, expecting to be met by a hail of bullets as we raced away from him. But his gun miraculously never even fired one shot!

The presence of God came into our vehicle in a special way. We made it home safely without being stopped by anyone else.

Although we did not actually see what pushed the drunk soldier away from our vehicle, I knew the angel of the Lord instantly arrived to take action when my wife called on the name of our Lord. That blessed angel removed the soldier from my path. I'm also convinced that the same angel kept us safe in the holy presence of the Lord during the rest of our journey home.

Did He not say that His angels would keep watch over us by day and by night? Whether or not we see them, they are always around exactly when we need them! Praise the Lord!

10

TWO ANGELS IN A TRUCK STOP?

This particular Sunday was a busy one. We had preached three services, with very little time between them. After the evening service, we went out to eat with the pastor. It was finally around midnight when we left their company and started out for our next destination.

We had an appointment early the next morning, so we were forced to travel all night to our next stop. When we travel like this my wife usually helps me drive and it is usually no problem to travel like this after church. But on this night my wife was so tired that she fell asleep almost as soon as we got started on our journey.

I had driven several hours until my eyes seemed to lose their focus and I was feeling cross-eyed. I was so sleepy that I was scaring myself, jerking awake at the last second before falling asleep at the wheel! Finally, I told myself that I just had to stop at the next restaurant or truck stop to get some coffee to try to wake up, so I could continue our journey to reach our appointment on time later that morning.

At the next exit, I saw a sign advertising a truck stop. As I pulled into the place I saw it wasn't a normal type of place where I usually would stop. It was an old stop, pretty much out of the way, and more than a bit run down. Entering the café, I went to the counter to order. I stammered and stuttered around until I finally got out that what I wanted was a large cup of coffee to go. I was literally leaning on the counter top, trying to stay awake and maintain my balance, when suddenly I had the urge to start looking around the gloomy interior of the cafe.

As I surveyed the room, my eyes fell on two young men sitting in a booth. They were eating and talking to each other. The thing that really attracted my attention was their clothing. They were out of place, not truck driver types, or the type of people that would be hanging around this type of establishment during the middle of the night. These two young men were very clean-cut, dressed in suits, looking like they had just come from church service somewhere.

As I was pondering this, I looked into the eyes of the young man that was facing me. That's when it happened!

A most unusual feeling came over me as I stood looking at this young man. He steadily stared directly at me, and I began to feel strength surging into my tired body. My mind came to full alertness, and I felt a renewing energy jolting through me like you wouldn't believe. I don't know how long I stood there looking into the eyes of the young man. Abruptly, the lady behind the counter handed me my coffee, taking my money to pay for it.

I was in a state of amazement and wonder as I carried the hot coffee back to our vehicle. My wife was still soundly asleep! When I got into the vehicle, what had happened in the cafe suddenly registered in my mind. As I started the motor of our car, I realize that I was totally refreshed and hadn't even taken a sip of the hot coffee!

Then the Word of the Lord came to my recollection, reminding me of the time when Jesus was in the wilderness fasting. After the devil left Him, the angel of the Lord came on the scene and strengthened Jesus. As I thought on this, the Holy Ghost spoke to me and said, "I did it then, I can do it now. I have given my angels charge over you to help you as you do your work for me."

I finished the trip in great spirits. I didn't feel tired again all night. I felt as though I had a whole night sleep, when in fact I have not slept even one wink! I reached our destination within the time set for the appointment and was very refreshed.

My spirit sang again, as it does now while I'm writing the story, that, "All day, all night, God's angels watching over me, my Lord!"

Isn't He wonderful to His heirs, His precious children? He has been so good to me and my wife, and even our children as we work for the Lord, both here in the US, and overseas.

When the angels are in charge, our security is certain!

11

THE ANGEL IMPARTS HOLINESS

The Atlanta metro-area crusade started in August 1995 and featured the Harvest of '96. It was initially sponsored by Reverend Donald L. Knight and the saints of DeKalb United Pentecostal Church. However, other metro-area pastors soon joined in the crusade efforts.

Soon after, special Saturday night crusade services were being held at various locations all around the metro area. The idea was to move the efforts of outreach outside the local churches, to neutral locations at area school auditoriums so more visitors would attend the Saturday night services.

The community area was saturated with prayer walks for several days before each crusade meeting. Promotional flyers were printed up and passed out on Saturday mornings before each crusade session. The teams passing out the tracts would also be praying as they worked. The area churches were praying at different times of day and night for these meetings.

At one crusade service, Pastor Joe was seated in the auditorium before the evening service. He was talking to the Lord in prayer when suddenly the Lord impressed him to go outside of the auditorium and invite people into the services. He went out and invited anyone, everyone, he saw. Whosoever he saw and invited went into the crusade and was baptized with the Holy Ghost!

Brother Joe invited one lady to enter the auditorium to visit the crusade service, and she did so. She entered, sat down, and immediately the Holy Spirit swept over her so powerfully that she began to weep. After a few minutes, she got up and left. Or so we thought. Instead, she went to the pay phone in the lobby and called home. She talked to her family, inviting them to come to the crusade. She told them to come and feel what she had found. Then she returned to the auditorium and waited until her family met her there.

When they arrived, she explained to them that she had been wandering around the city, praying to the Lord to show her how to preserve her family. They were on the verge of breaking up over internal family conflicts. She was on the edge of the having a nervous breakdown over the worry and strain of her family crisis.

Then, she later told us, this strange man (Brother Joe) walked up to her near the school and begin to talk to her about special services that night. He urged her to attend and let God minister to her. He said to her that he just knew that God had a miracle for her that night! So, she went to the service.

As she whispered to her family while the service was going on, explaining to them what had happened to her, something swept over them, just as it had done over her before they arrived. They also begin to weep. Trained altar workers begin to move in to help them pray, and all six of them were filled with the Holy Ghost as the service was stopped to pray for them.

The mother testified of this story publicly afterward. She said that "something" had touched her after she came into the service. She was so "touched" that she began to cry and ask God to forgive her and her family for their sins and to save them.

We believe an angel touched her after she came into that service. And we also believe that an angel touched her family after they arrived at the service. And we know that the presence of our Holy Lord certainly saved her and her family because He filled all six of them with the Holy Ghost that very night! When they left the school auditorium they had new attitudes and the anointing of the Living God in their lives to make them the family they were supposed to be.

The preaching of the Gospel is left to men, but God sends His angels to cause hungry souls to be directed towards us while we're doing his work. Praises unto His holy name forever and ever!

12

BRO. JOE IS NOT AN ANGEL

At the same crusade service as the previous testimony, another event happened that is worth sharing.

Brother Joe was still out in the surrounding areas near the school auditorium, inviting people to come into the Crusade services. He's a dedicated worker who really loves the Lord, and not just in word. He's willing to work, witness, pray, fast, or whatever, for the great cause. While others were inside sitting down, taking it easy, Brother Joe was earnestly hunting for "one more" lost sheep to bring to the service!

One lady was stopped on the road, as she drove her car! The man that stopped her said that if she would go inside the building where the services being held, God would do something special for her. She agreed to go to the service, so she turned her car into the parking lot. She parked her automobile and entered the school auditorium. As she entered the service, the Holy Ghost began to deal with her and she soon began earnestly to call on the Lord in prayer. The trained altar workers moved in and begin to pray with her. Within minutes she received the baptism of the Holy Ghost!

Afterward, she wanted to find the man who invited her into the crusade service, so she could offer her thanks for his help in pointing her to the wonderful spiritual blessing God had just given her in the service. The ushers directed her to Brother Joe, who was the only man outside the auditorium inviting people in the area to the meeting.

She quickly said, "No! That's not the man who invited me." Again, she started to look for him. But after she looked over the entire crowd that night, she realized that it must have been an angel of the Lord who had told her to come in and to receive something from the Lord. No one else fit the physical description she offered of the one who invited her into the service! She went on her way rejoicing because angels were watching over her and helped usher her into the kingdom of God.

To God be the glory, for the great things he has done!

13

THE ANGEL HOLDUP

We were on a year of deputation travel, on our way to a church service one evening. You know how it is when you're running close on time? That's usually when things start to go haywire, right? So, on this night, I was carefully trying to make every minute count on our journey towards our destination.

Approaching an intersection, the light turned green for us, when all of a sudden, the car in front of us stopped in the middle of our lane. The car just sat there blocking us, so that we couldn't continue with our journey. There was no way for us to go around the vehicle because of the intersection and the oncoming traffic.

I was quickly growing upset at the driver of the car because it appeared there was no apparent reason for him to stop like that! I immediately began to calculate a "pedal to the metal" move to accelerate around the halted car that was blocking us. Without warning another car appeared, traveling at a very high speed, and passed through the intersection in front of us. Had we not been stopped by the vehicle in front of us, we would have been broadsided by the speeding vehicle. At the speed at which he was going, most likely, all of us in our vehicle would have been killed!

When the realization of what had just happened hit us, we were very shaken up. It took a few minutes to calm and collect ourselves because it was so apparent that we had just been spared death or serious maiming.

Finally, we proceeded through the now clear intersection toward the church where we were scheduled for our meeting that night. As we got to the intersection, I realize that whoever was in the stalled car had probably just saved our lives. I looked in every direction for the car that had stopped so abruptly in front of us. To our amazement, the car had disappeared!

We had all seen it. We were all getting frustrated at the driver of that car. But friends, it was instantly gone when the danger passed, and none of us saw it drive away, or where it went! There wasn't even any argument between us, everybody in the car was happy to agree that an angel had stopped the car just to save our lives!

Again, the Lord had ministered to our hearts and lives. He helped us to understand anew that he has given charge to his angels,

For it is written, he shall give his angels charge concerning thee: lest at any time thou dash thy foot against a stone. (Matthew 4:6)

Or, God will also give charge to his angels to guard us even against an oncoming vehicle sent by an enemy to try to destroy us and stop our work for God. Those familiar words came back to me again from the old song, "Angels watching over me, my Lord!"

Oh, that men everywhere would praise Him for His goodness and mercy towards men. Thank You, Lord Jesus!

14

ANGELS CONQUER THE AIRPORT

The Lord spoke to me that Satan was gathering spiritual forces on the eastern coast of the United States in preparation for the 1996 Olympics that would be held in Atlanta. The Olympic Games were to be the kickoff of the new spiritual offensive against the eastern seaboard of the United States that Satan was planning against the church of the Living God. The Lord also spoke by visions to an evangelist from Baltimore, Maryland, who was visiting the Atlanta metro area while he was holding a revival meeting in Newnan, Georgia. The Lord impressed him with the knowledge that the airport held the key to defeating those huge numbers of evil immigrating spirits.

Then the Lord spoke to Brother Bill Brooks, who serves as our administrator at International Relief Services, concerning how to erect spiritual barriers that would totally stop the massive spiritual immigration of evil and warring spirits. The Lord even gave him specific prayers to pray at the airport that the Lord promised to honor.

None of the three of us communicated what we had heard from the Lord until we came together several days later to discuss what each felt was occurring spiritually in the area of Metro Atlanta Crusade.

I felt led of the Lord to call a prayer walk for all men who were considered Street Warriors during the Atlanta Metro Crusade and asked the evangelist and Brother Brooks to accompany me to Hartsfield International Airport in Southwest Atlanta, on a Saturday morning in February of 1996.

The morning we were to meet at the airport at 10 a.m., a big snowstorm (which is very rare for Atlanta) struck the city and shut down virtually all travel. The roads were solid sheets of ice. Travel was almost totally halted throughout the Metro Area.

Some of the brothers got to the airport by riding the commuter train. Most, however, didn't even try to travel through the snow, ice, and bitter cold. But since International Relief Services headquarters is only 25 miles Southwest from the airport, we decided to try to get there. There were some heavy patches of ice on I-85, but we made it to the airport by about 10:50 a.m. However, we never did see any of the other brothers who were supposed to meet us there!

As we began to walk and pray in the airport, Brother Brooks separated from the evangelist and me, walking around the North

Terminal baggage area, around to the north MARTA Train Station, then met us again back at the South Baggage Terminal. As he turned from the main lobby and passed by the North Baggage Terminal, he heard what sounded like voices of several of the brethren from the Stone Mountain Church laughing and singing some church choruses. He turned to find them, but never did see even one of them!

Continuing around the North Terminal, toward where he was to meet the evangelist and me, as he turned the very North corner of the Baggage Terminal, he heard a voice behind him, near the exit, say, "That's Brother Brooks! He's part of the prayer team." When he turned to see who was speaking, thinking it was one or more of the brothers who were supposed to meet us for the prayer walk, he got a major surprise. No one was there! Who was singing the chorus and talking, he asked himself, as he continued walking and praying. Brother Brooks said it was the angels stationed at each place by the Lord.

The three of us joined forces again in the Baggage Terminal Lobby and approached the main security area that leads to the escalators going down to the lower level transit trains, which move passengers to the various flight terminals for the arrivals and departures. As we approached the security gates, suddenly all three of us saw a heavily-armed phalanx or warrior angels running ahead of us, fanning out through the security area. It appeared they were clearing the way for us as we walked and prayed!

We continued praying for a total of more than 4 hours. Every major entry port and exit port in that airport was walked through and prayed over. And according to the instructions we had received from the Lord, spiritual security gates (angels stationed at each place) were erected that prevented evil spirits from entering through any of these ports. Inbound, evil spiritual forces were forced to stop at the spiritual security gates and return to their origination points. This prevented a rotation of fresh spiritual troops fighting against our saints in the churches.

Our Crusade Intercessors and prayer warriors prayed and interceded with God until they defeated the evil spiritual forces of Satan in those community areas throughout the city. Then Satan would rotate his defeated troops out and replace them with fresh troops from European and former communistic nations, and our saints would have to begin the spiritual battle all over again. This very diabolic strategy was devised to keep our people warring without gaining the confidence of victory!

However, the spiritual security gates we erected at the instructions of the Lord, kept the defeated local evil spirits in place and prevented their leaving. This meant they had to continue trying to fight our praying saints without rest or time to recuperate!

The culmination of this victory occurred at the International Terminal. As all three of us sat praying in front of the US Customs security gates, through which every single international passenger must pass to enter the United States through the Atlanta airport, suddenly another flight of angels moved into the area and took up positions. It was amazing, in that all of us saw them. They looked fearsome and ready for war.

After resting a while in the comfortable seats in the International Terminal, we left the airport, assured that God had indeed locked down the airport to prevent extra-curricular spiritual travel by Satan's forces.

That night the weather temperatures dropped drastically across the entire United States! So many low-temperature records were set, that the newspapers were filled with reports the next morning. It was eerie! Atlanta set a record for cold temperatures that were an all-time weather history record!

Greater spiritual victories were gained in the Metro Atlanta Crusade after that event. Virtually every visitor entering the crusade services received the baptism of Holy Ghost during the services. So many water baptisms were occurring that leaders began to take them to separate rooms for personal Bible studies, then provide a baptismal clothing, and they were baptized while the services continued. If a person had not received the Holy Ghost before entering the water, they received it while being baptized.

It was absolutely amazing. And God is still in the business of making these things happen in other cities, if the people are willing.

Even yours!

15

WESTERN UNION MESSAGE FROM HEAVEN

The following story was related to me by Reverend William C. Brooks, a former pastor in Raleigh, North Carolina, where Brother Wayne Huntley now pastors. Brother Brooks now serves as the Administrator at the International Relief Services, Inc.

Brother Brooks was on a 10-day total fast (no food, only water) with Rev. Irvin Baxter Jr., pastor in Richmond, Indiana. They were staying at a farmhouse belonging to Brother Baxter's father, near the Indiana-Ohio state line in Eastern Central Indiana.

On the evening of the sixth day, Brother Brooks became disturbed. He felt empty, alone, and abandoned. He said he could not feel the presence of the Lord and felt he needed help. He called several pastor friends by telephone and asked them to pray for him, informing them of his fast, and some of the particulars concerning the reason for the fast. They, of course, stated that they and the congregations they pastored would offer up prayer on behalf of Brother Brooks, asking the Lord for a spiritual breakthrough.

The guest bedroom where Brother Brooks was sleeping had a door off the main hallway of the house, and a second door that led into a bathroom jointly serving the bedroom and the kitchen.

After the telephone conversations, Brother Brooks retired to his room, spending time in prayer and Bible study before going to sleep. It was close to midnight or a bit after when he turned out the lights and went to sleep.

The next morning, at promptly 5 a.m., which was the seventh day of the fast, a man walked through the wall next to the hallway door and stood at the foot of the bed where Brother Brooks was sleeping. Coming wide awake, he said up in bed, scared, somewhat confused, but looking for an exit to get out of the room in a big hurry!

The man was tall and muscular. He was dressed in a Western Union uniform like the Western Union telegram deliverers wore when Brother Brooks was a young boy, growing up in Michigan City, Indiana. The man wore a little round leather cap and had a leather pouch that was attached to a large leather strap that hung cross-ways over his shoulder, the bag hanging at his right side, at a hip length.

Brother Brooks bolted straight up in the bed, glaring bug-eyed at the man. The visitor looked him right in the eyes, and spoke firmly, and said to him, "I have a message for you from God."

With those words he reached into the leather pouch and pulled out a piece of paper, about letter sized, folded in half, just like the old home-delivered Western Union telegrams. The man opened the sheet of paper, holding it with one hand on the top and on the other hand at the bottom. When it was fully opened, he extended his arms toward Brother Brooks, who was still somewhat paralyzed, sitting up straight as an arrow in the bed.

Suddenly the message began to grow. It grew until it miraculously covered the entire wall of the room where the hallway door entered the bedroom. The messenger disappeared behind the huge message on the wall!

Brother Brooks read the message. It read: "I have told you before that I would never leave you nor forsake you. I tell you again, I will never leave you nor forsake you. Trust in Me. I will be with you always, even into the end. Wait on me." There was no signature, but with an understanding, Brother Brooks said that he already knew who the message was from!

Skin crawling, hair standing up, Brother Brooks felt like he was just about to fall apart and lose control of himself. The man calmly flipped the paper back into a double-fold. He reached down, lifted the flap on the letter message pouch, and dropped the message inside. Then, still disdaining the door, he turned, walked back through the wall and disappeared.

Leaping from the bed, running to the door, Brother Brooks

quickly open it to see if the man was there. He was gone. A check of the entire house proved that the visitor was nowhere to be found!

Without a doubt, Brother Brooks said, it was an angel from the Lord that brought the Heavenly message of assurance. God cares intensely about His children and will go to great lengths to let us know that He is with all of His children and will never abandon us.

It may be that we do not understand some of the things that happened to us, but God is our Helper and Friend if we are His. And He is always present with us.

> *"For in Him we live, and move, and have our being; as certain also as our own poets have said, For we are also his offspring." (Acts 17:28)*

As the Psalmist said,

> *"Mine enemies would swallow me up; for they be many that fight against me O Lord Most High. What time I am afraid, I will trust in Thee. In God I will praise His word, in God I will put my trust; I will not fear what flesh can do unto me." (Psalms 56:2-4).*

Again, in the New Testament, the Bible declares,

"For He hath said, I will never leave thee, nor forsake thee. So that we may boldly say, The Lord is my Helper, and I will not fear what man shall do unto me." (Hebrews 13:5).

16

ANGELS ON THE SWITCHBOARD

I had barely reached my threescore-and-ten when an unbelievable incident occurred in my life.

I had been extremely busy with ministry connections, but I was feeling tired and exhausted. One morning in my prayer I told God that I'm willing to do anything, but I needed some type of supernatural touch to give me the strength that I needed to complete the task at hand. I knew He would answer my prayer and I knew that I would receive strength, but I had no idea how this was going to take place.

I had started my day and gone to Lowe's Hardware to pick up some plumbing items to help with the work that I was doing for that day. When I reached the back of the store where the plumbing supplies were displayed, I suddenly had a strong burning in my chest. I stopped for a moment and leaned over against the counter trying to catch my breath. For a moment it released just a little bit, but I knew I was in danger, so I headed toward the front of the store.

Just before I reached the front of the store it hit again, but this time more severe. There was a shopping cart just in front of me and I actually grabbed the cart and bent over, trying to maintain consciousness and overcome the fire burning in my chest. I knew I was in trouble and felt very certain that I was having a heart attack. I did not know what to do and I couldn't straighten up. Fear began to grip me and I cried out for God to help me. No sooner had those words left my lips than my cell phone started to ring. I answered the cell phone and to my amazement my cousin Wayne Huntley was on the other end of the line. I exclaimed, "Wayne, pray for me! I'm having a heart attack," and immediately he went into prayer and I started to feel a change coming over me.

I straightened up, made my way to the cashier to pay for my purchases, went out, and got in the car and started my way back to my house. On the way home, I called my wife and told her that I was having a heart attack and I was coming home. She in turn called my son-in-law Rob Harris, who immediately came to my house by the time I got home. I took a bath and dressed and he took me to the emergency room.

It was in the emergency room, after they finally got me settled down that they realize that I was, in fact, having a heart attack. They immediately started running tests and found out that I had major blockages and wanted to transfer me to Atlanta to a heart hospital where they were going to perform open heart surgery on me.

The funny thing is that the day after I was going to do my little project I was going to go to Atlanta to the heart hospital to visit my uncle who was having open heart surgery that day.

Little did I know that I would end up in the hospital with him having open heart surgery by the same doctor that performed the surgery on him.

The amazing thing was this was the best heart surgeon in the whole area and he was completely booked up weeks in advance for a surgery. But, amazing as it may seem, someone canceled, and they were able to get me in immediately and he completed a completely successful 5-bypass surgery on me.

It wasn't until after the surgery, during my recuperation time, that I had a chance to call Brother Huntley and thank him for praying for me. He thanked me for calling him and said he was more than willing to respond to my request. I told Wayne, "I didn't call you. My phone rang when I was in the middle of this heart attack."

He said to me, "I didn't call you either. My phone rang, and I picked it up and it was you asking me to pray for you because you were having a heart attack."

We both paused for a moment trying to make some sense out of what had occurred and finally come to realize that it was a supernatural connection that was made not on my part, and not on his part, but somehow the angel of the Lord took control of the switchboard and supernaturally connected us. The request was made, the prayer was given, and the miracle took place.

As I travel down memory lane and put pen to paper, I am reminded at 73 years old that God is still faithful and he has placed in the ER for our benefit, ministering spirits to the heirs of salvation. It is unbelievable what they are able to do if we just trust Him and believe that His angels are truly watching over us!

ABOUT THE AUTHOR

Johnny Wayne Garrison was born in Concord, North Carolina, in 1944. He became a Christian in 1962. A double blessing fell upon his life in 1963: he married Peggy Joyce Padgett and began to preach the Gospel of Jesus Christ. The Garrisons, soon a growing family (daughter Candi, and son Mark Andrew), received full appointment as missionaries to Nigeria, West Africa, in 1975. There, he served as superintendent of missionary work in Nigeria, and in neighboring Cameroon.

J. W. Garrison was the founder and president of the Christian Development Center of Nigeria, a Bible and Technical   college for training national ministers. The Garrisons currently reside in Moreland, Georgia, a sleepy little town about 30 minutes southwest of Atlanta. Moreland is the headquarters of International Relief Services, Incorporated, of which J. W. Garrison is the founder and current International Director. The International Relief Services, Inc., is an independent organization that serves missionaries in need. Their basic purpose is to assist missionaries located anywhere in the world with whatever they feel they need, but which is not provided in their regular budgets. The International Relief Services' motto is, "We deliver relief to the whole world."

Made in the USA
Columbia, SC
17 July 2023

20572770R00045